flyposter
frenzy

FLYPOSTER FRENZY posters from the anticopyright network
Compiled and with an introduction by Matthew Fuller.

Design by Matthew Fuller, cover designed with Simon Pope,
photography by Mandie Beuzeval.

First published 1992 by Working Press, 85 St Agnes Place, Kennington
London SE11 4BB

Printed by Total Central Limited, 4 Farnham Royal, Kennington Lane, Vauxhall
London SE11 5RG

**Copyright of all aspects of this book remains with the individual producers
but is waived for non-profit reproduction**

Due to the nature of the project there are some posters distributed by the network
and reproduced in this book that we don't know the original producers of. If you
have produced any of these posters without being credited please get in touch

ISBN 1 870736 15 X

British Library Cataloguing-in-Publication Data
A catalogue record for this book is available from the British Library

ACKNOWLEDGEMENTS: Thanks are due to everyone who has contributed to the development of anticopyright and to this book and who collectively are its authors. To everyone, too many to name, who ever designed or stuck up a poster, made a donation, helped with publicity, got in contact with ideas or questions, acted as a distribution point or whatever... Thanks.

ANTICOPYRIGHT DISTRIBUTION POINTS

C/O 70 HIGH STREET, LEICESTER, LEICESTERSHIRE, UK

PO BOX 406, STOKE-ON-TRENT, STAFFORDSHIRE, ST1 4RN, UK

BOX15, 52 CALL LANE, LEEDS, WEST YORKSHIRE, LS1 6DT, UK

PO BOX 368, CARDIFF, CF2 1SQ, WALES, UK

PO BOX 5975, CHICAGO, IL 60680-5975, USA

contents

ade l. vice   ade l. vice   anonymous

anonymous   anonymous   fagagaga   hakim bey   institute of fatuous research   institute of fatuous research

   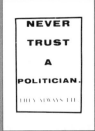  

institute of fatuous research   institute of fatuous research   institute of fatuous research   anonymous   clifford harper   anonymous

kian de la couer   museum of modern alienation   mr. social control   anonymous   anonymous   anonymous

 allan finlay

 anonymous

 anonymous

 matthew fuller

 matthew fuller

 domino

 john

 penny kemps

chris b.

graham c.

 class war

 mark pawson

 mark pawson

 feminist terrorist tourists

 anonymous

 anonymous

 totally normal

 totally normal

 totally normal

 clemente padin

 clemente padin

 maurice burns

 anonymous

raising hell | anonymous | anonymous | liz | fuel and transport advisory commitee | fuel and transport advisory commitee

    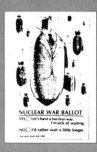 

anonymous | anonymous | anonymous | anonymous | anonymous | act up

doug minkler | doug minkler | doug minkler | eleutheros productions | eleutheros productions | eleutheros productions

eleutheros productions | karen eliot | jenny holzer | jenny holzer | anti-fascist action | anonymous

i.m.i.   anonymous   xeroxial endarchy   avpm   anonymous   t.o.p.y. heart

guerrilla girls   guerrilla girls   gone wild   john yates   anonymous

anti-authoritarians anonymous   meloni   anonymous   dave smith   perry coma   anonymous

anonymous   anonymous   marion coutts   homocult   homocult

flyposter frenzy

GRUDGE-U-LIKE... No copy of this book should have its spine unbroken! Ram the bastard down against the copier glass until it replicates itself in fear. It's designed to be used and with its handy pick your own gripe format there's something for everyone. Balance yourself out - get a chip on both shoulders, then broadcast the fact to your friends, neighbours workmates and enemies by plastering copies of these posters all over the place.

Photocopiers - interplanetary saviours from another dimension?

The invention of the photocopier as a tool for bureaucrats and businessmen, facilitating the cheap, swift and accurate reproduction of documents doesn't immediately conjure up the prospect of a powerful tool for subversion. Office workers everywhere know using it as the ultimate in shitwork. The machine makes weird smells, annoying noises and using it usually gets dumped into the thrill packed life of the kid on the training scheme along with making the tea and tidying up.

The photocopy's status as a cultural artifact, as art, doesn't get much more glamourous. The quality is harsh, the paper's frail and after a while even this deteriorates. Instead of preciousness and collectability the photocopy remains steadfastly valueless and disposable.

It is exactly these qualities which make the photocopier a useful medium. Most people have access to a photocopier either at work or in one of the copy bureaus that can be found on every high street. Unlike other printing methods it doesn't require much skill to get a result. There's no training required, and what you see on your paste-up is usually pretty close to what comes out, reassuringly warmed, at the other end of the machine. Copies can be made as and when required rather than being optimistically mass-produced only to spend the next decade yellowing gracefully at the back of someone's cupboard - and what time is sweeter than company time - when being spent producing weirdo literature using the company's paper?

In *The Work of Art in the Age of its Mechanical Reproducibility* Walter Benjamin first detailed the gradual elimination of "aura" - the "unique phenomenon of distance however close it may be" from works of art as mechanical processes of reproduction, particularly photography and film, superseded the devotional contemplation of the unique object. He charted this transition from the singular to the mass-produced as an inevitable technological progression. This transition should not only be noted and adapted to, but extended until the reification of "aura" and notions of originality are surpassed entirely. The photocopier, along with the image manipulating computer, the sampler and other fab products of the evil multinationals throws the roles of producer, reproducer, user, into confusion. Who can tell which photocopy is an original? The negation of these traditional artistic values opens culture up to a freeing of creative activity.

Being multiple and never unique the photocopy is always social. Even if only a single copy exists at any one point it is always possible to instantly produce hundreds of others with exactly the same (lack of) aura. Some of the posters in this book have been used, copied and passed on by people until no one can remember who did it originally - hence all the anonymous ones.

This lack of aura makes the photocopy less easily distinguishable as an "artistic object". The copiers' constant use in the production of authoritative documents for large inflexible structures such as corporations or local government allows the misattribution of documents to these sources when their style is mimicked making this authority all the easier to undermine. (For instance at the time of the Gulf War thousands of fake and piss-taking call up papers were sent to unsuspecting people by their friends. Re-copied and passed on by them in turn, they got all over the country really fast.) The posters here that take on the look of adverts or official announcements go one step further than the t-shirts and other clothes that pirate the logos and look of clothes by major labels and designers. While these are subversive in that you'd have to be an idiot to buy the "real thing" when you can get a copy down the market for a quarter of the price, they rely on - if only for sales, the sustained popularity of the original that they will always remain in the shadow of. Here, once the posters have appropriated the look they turn cannibal and go straight for the jugular.

The blurring of source that becomes available with this technology points toward an advancement of culture as accumulative. That is to say that all "innovations" are built on the sum total of what has gone before. All developments are seen as the enrichment of the collective sum rather than sporadic bursts of genius. (The development of the photocopier itself being a prime example of the fusion and adaption of previously separated technologies.) The hyperinflation in the value of the "original" sinks lived culture into an inertia refuted by Lautreamont's, Situationist apropriated, slogan "Plagiarism is necessary. Progress implies it."

Lighting up the streets in glorious black + white

Flyposters have provided a cultural form which those on the fringes of, or totally outside dominant cultures, have been able to use with great effect. The uses have varied from person to person and from situation to situation. The common characteristic is that flyposters are a medium for groups or individuals with little money or access to the established media. They are exciting, dangerous and subversive.

The anticopyright network was founded to make a large number of these posters available and to create an open space for the development of the poster as a creative and agitational form. Anticopyright has roots in the "underground" but aims to exist aboveground and in conflict with a culture that attempts to reduce us all to ciphers.

Flyposter Frenzy reproduces ninety of the posters that we have collected over the past three years. There are two reasons for producing it: Firstly to make these posters, which are some of the most popular ones from our catalogue, available and ready for use to a wider range of people and secondly to intensify the debate around interventional cultural practice in public spaces.

In recent years groups and artists that are not only highly literate in "high culture" but ready and willing to manipulate the language of the media and other cultures have sprung up. The best known of these are; Jenny Holzer, Barbera Kruger and the graphics collectives of ACT-UP as well as the Guerrilla Girls and OUTPOST. We will be presenting work by some of these alongside material that has never been connected with mainstream art discourse, work from other traditions, other genealogies, but that has immense importance in the consideration of possibilities for cultural practice today. Anticopyright connects with this new media practice but also with it's flip side; manifestos, broadsheets, montages, pranks, disinformation and with the necessity of constructing political and cultural activity in the face of important and immediate threats such as homelessness, racism, the destruction of ecologies and so on.

The book will appeal to those who are interested in the creation of a vital oppositional culture but also to those on whose behalf both theorists and political militants are wont to wax most lyrical. This book is by and for those who have been marginalised but whose lives and their manifestations of them, in this case as posters, are central to any project which seeks to understand or to change.

Public space - common ground

The flyposter's intervention in public space, in physical terms, disruption, is minimal. It is almost gone as soon as it is placed. Forming a shifting, fluctuating second skin on the city its effectivity is in direct conflict with the notions of permanence, eternal verity and worth that clutter our towns in the form of monuments. Monuments built to withstand the passing of time, attempting to impose a fixed, everlasting image. The flyposter formalises a necessary impermanence - it's brief presence attempting to stimulate the viewer into self activity by denying itself fixity, interested in diffusion and not central points. The flyposter asks the viewer of itself "What is it? Who made it and why?" Its function is to destabilise the cohesion of what we are told about cities and to insert itself as a temporary site of antagonism, whether as part of a specific and broader movement with well defined political or cultural aims or for the sheer joy of rupturing power's smooth transmission of meaning and death.

Those posters that do articulate specific social and political contentions are not restricted by an adhesion to a particular organisation or "line". This has allowed a wide variety of uses, from community groups concerned with getting better housing or beating racists and fascists out of their areas to individuals concerned to do some civic minded shit-stirring.

- or battleground?

Public space is a myth. The last of the common land was bundled up and sealed a long time ago. In cities and industrialised nature every last millimetre is so obviously owned by, broadcast to, and fought over by a deluge of competing interests. Public space remains contingent on what and who is excluded or included by definitions of a mythical "general public". In contrast to "public art", whose practitioners must always have one eye cocked to what is required by this constituency the flyposter is unabashedly conflictual. This conflictuality is unavoidable for anyone who has experienced the city in slightly different terms to that of a literary exercise; as a place of traffic, accidents, violence, lust, strength, poverty, intoxication, attacks, hunger, fear and shopping…

Flyposters and the Quality Environment

Flyposters are generally placed within an architectural environment, consequently it is worthwhile to consider the functions of architectures in relation to informational and behavioural discourses and the ways in which these are subverted and repositioned. Social and cultural positionings work in material and spatial terms. Posters counterpose points of view in real terms, as cultural constructs they are something tangible, having an effectivity shaping contexts and frameworks, points of view and points of conflict. They interlace orientations of struggle, challenge acquiescence and the provoke the revelation of intentions and desires.

Arrangements of built environments must also be seen in terms of symbolic power relations which by their denial or allowance of possibility may be equally harrowing or liberating. Public space as idealized on behalf of the general public has become the shopping centre. The mythology presented in shopping centres such as Cardiff's Capitol Exchange or Birmingham's Palisades with their strange mixtures of film set, local vernacular, art deco or Victorian play bricks embody an official postmodernism. Entirely ephemeral, buildings gorging on their own display, which when you enter, credit card in hand, become immense pleasure domes of consumption. Displayed commodities draw the crowds together in high-security safety, cocooned from the street. The momementary pleasure of buying is connected successfully with the lack of lack; no political demonstrations, no beggars no violence. Seduced by a thousand special effects and fortified by a snack from one of the range of themed eateries the abandonment is delayed. That was a couple of years ago, before the boutiques started emptying, when people no longer somehow managed to afford Belgian chocolates and designer socks. However, the project - the channelling of desires into an endless and well monitored one room labyrinth, remains the same.

Every Reality a Virtual Reality

The apparent permanence of buildings; concrete, glass, steel, is constantly repositioned by non-tangible information systems; electronic imaging, surveillance equipment, communications structures and so on. The seemingly natural and always "necessary" authority of the architect and client is an attempted channelling of social currents whose flow cannot help but burst its banks. Architecture is reinterpreted by shifts and conflicts within social structure. Even the subjectivity of its inception's form cannot remain a functional constant; Churches become housing, warehouses become homes for the rich, paving stones shatter windows. The Bauhaus idea of a homogenised form and function, the semiotic value fused with the utilitarian - the signifier coupled with a conveniently immediate signified was produced by a discourse dominated by a self-proclaimed rationality. They knew that transformations of social life could be made by way of the transformation of space but they couldn't countenance contradiction. The voice of the author commanding the interpretation and use of the building only in terms of the denotative attempted to drown out the connotations of the user. Conversely the self consciously irrational and *weird* novelty architect relies as much on this concept of the rational for effect as he equals its hectoring voice. The sham colloquialisms and classicisms of much postmodern architecture embody the compression of history into that of a monological vision.

The civic improvement developments that encrust our pavements and walls along seems of financial movement are renamed in the great spirit of democracy as public art. The class alliances that place these edifices to the blandness of the official mind, symbols of the supposed unity, historically and in the present, of a carved up terrain, stifle difference with the clammy hand of homogeneity.

Combined; the multivalent spectacle, a regime of flexible accumulation - the spectacle as play and the spectacle of posturing civic "health" reinforce each other. This false plurality and arrogant sports centre virility attempt to smother diversity and confrontation. The flyposter does not only erode the bombast of architecture - it is architecture - an anarchitecture.

No doubt some of these flyposters are ending up providing variations on the James Dean/Marilyn Monroe/ Fluffy Kitten poster as decorations for people's rooms rather than being splattered up on a wall in a glorious blow against the commodification of art, or something. But this can be easily understood when you realise that when correctly placed in the bedroom they will improve the quality of sex and in the kitchen, the taste of cooking.

people in any of its processes shown by the state results in the dismissal of any political ideas and action all together.

We are not looking for any kind of final resolution to these problems, or any of the others that are faced by people producing flyposters, nor do we believe that in themselves they form anything more than contingencies, that in every situation the conditions will differ and that everything is possible to deal with on that basis. We can in fact use them to our advantage.

The stale, same old lies of democracy can be used as a trope for the language of a refreshing and vital "real politics". While the dully frantic screams of "SMASH THIS! FIGHT THAT!" will no doubt go on for ever on some faction's mental barricades there will always be eruptions of humour and inspiring demands for the impossible and the necessary. It is to the defiant and unexpected, breaks with received "reality", that we look for development.

Advertising is essentially always fragile and subject to constant rupture by peoples' expectations and intelligence. Advertising attempts to endow the merchandise with potency, make its purchase and

Advertising and sloganeering

While Anticopyright has provided a forum for the discussion and development of flyposting as a cultural and political form there remain various issues around what is possible to be done within this format; whether complex ideas can be effectively put across/ whether didactic sloganeering ever achieves anything, whether media saturation reduces everything to just another advertisement, or whether the total disregard for involving

TOP TIPS FOR HOT FLYPOSTING ACTION

If you feel like pampering yourself a little bit why not try mixing your glue with warm water?

Put your glue in two carrier bags. That way, if one leaks, the other will catch it. It also doesn't look quite as dodgy as romping round the place with a big bucket of what looks like elephant sperm.

Go in twos or threes, it's more of a laugh and that way the one who isn't busy putting up glue or posters at that moment can keep a look out.

Big brushes are genuinely better and more time saving than smaller ones. The real connossieurs use paint rollers to put their glue on with.

Once you've slapped the glue up and put the posters on top of it, make sure you give them another brushing over to push the air bubbles and creases out. This makes them harder to tear down.

Daytime is as good a time as any to go out, no one really cares what you get up to and people are more likely to ask you for a copy of the poster than give you any hassle. If anyone does, just tell them you're on a council training scheme, make up a phone number and tell them any old name for a council official - your "superviser" to get in touch with at that number.

consumption inseparable from the exciting and sexualised images that accompany it. The purpose of these posters is not simply the unnecessary reverse; to make excitement and sexuality™ desirable rather than the product. Advertising attempts a channelling of desire and in channelling desire does not merely repress it but focuses it, enables it to *achieve* the merchandise. Its supplications are orders. The purpose, if it can be called that, of these posters is to destroy this imposition, diffuse this focussing and in doing so flood out beyond these channels.

We can learn from the techniques of advertising, adapt it, wreck it. How can we not do so, it constructs our environment. This is getting back to nature. It is

content - you need only to compare the length of the text of advertisements in underground train stations compared to those on billboards to notice this. People have a lot of time to read at bus stops for instance. Just because the content of the poster has to be communicated in seconds does not immediately rule out anything but the inane. It does however mean that we need to be careful of stripping language down, simplifying it so that it becomes rigid, lacking in idiosyncrasy and beauty. The ironic, use of density and lightness, the scraping and pasting of accumulated layers of signs, dislocation, are means by which fixed meanings, from us or onto us, are overcome.

Higher Purpose + the mechanisms of authority.

Whether these posters interrogate and disperse the language of authority or just plain slag it off ("Never trust a politician - they always lie") they all celebrate its downfall. Universal languages and their inherent promise of "rational" discourses, in the pursuit of reform, have become an irrelevance no matter how much they are grasped for by the fast fading avatars of "progress". There's no need to bemoan this loss of a "common language", of rationality. Because loss for us it certainly isn't. Universal languages have never meant anything in the way of a shared experience but a decoding device for those who situate themselves and only themselves, at axial points of power in society. Their translation to us of our own lives into that of a general public is increasingly hard to dissimulate. Between those included or excluded from the post-industrial game plan lies a massive disproportion of wealth in what has become the prime commodity and currency - informations. Society can no longer be held together by appeals to a common discourse, a greater good. Increasingly conflict has no mediation in appeals to some mythic common ground because it is precisely this common ground that is slipping away. We are being left to act out the role of general public while capital migrates into the abstract and its attendants attempt to enforce a scorched earth in its wake.

For anyone who actually gives a toss whether this is **art** or **agit-prop**.
- If the difference is that art is involved in making form problematical then all the work here is. It's just that most of it aims at making, not just it's own, but the whole of society's form problematical. To say the least.

useful to study and use the array of visual and textual devices that are used in advertising. Firstly, they did not originate there, they are culled from techniques that develop from all kinds of situations, they are not immediately compromised when used elsewhere and secondly, they work.

The danger of oversimplifying the issues that these posters involve themselves in is always present and undoubtedly there are some here that will not satisfy some people in this respect. The fact that posters have only about two or three seconds while people are walking past them in the street in which to be noticed is not an intractable limitation. The placing of posters is often just as important as their

Only Global Niceness Can Save Us Now

"Committal" chosen from an arbitrary check-list of right on concerns makes no essential change. The martian artists who land in sections of human society bleeping "solidarity with the underprivileged" and the revolutionary cabals who emerge at moments of struggle with ideologies to sell inevitably end up coming to terms with their failure with the platitude that we're all "alienated". Yeah, sure we are. Is it beside the point that this alienation can be measured in direct proportion to their love the people - help the people - art for the people specialisation? The quantifications with which people are referred to in "progressive" cultural work, idealist though they may be, can never be anything but quantifications. The panicking lack of "the masses", "the public", and "society" as an audience that hits the virtuous like the threat of Hell is a result of their refusal to see the "audience" as anything but passive. Creative production of meanings through engagement with cultures is a threat to the author (of any ideological persuasion) at centre stage.

The leftist (or artist) specialist identity is formed by the role as oppositional to the way authority is conducted by those who hold the dominant position. This role is performed in order to mask the specialist as integral to the dominant term. As the structure loses the intactness of its fake pluralism they lose their role as oppositional. Their complicity reveals itself. History is not the history of class struggle until on the level of the individual's subjective engagements these engagements accumulate into social formations, a collective subject. Instead of the arduous efforts of these cultural workers to be "pro-oppressed" and "anti-hegemonic" they should determine and alter the relations and conditions of themselves and their peers and thus *embody* rather than represent displacement of oppression and hegemony.

Simple machine

The way in which the anticopyright network is structured is designed to make it as accessible as possible. We work on a principle of decentralization. Each distribution point is relatively independent, responsible for raising its own funds and supplying posters and any information to people who get in contact. The catalogue that lists the posters is of course the same for all of the distribution points in order to avoid any muddles. We also use the same basic design for the general publicity leaflets which briefly explain what anticopyright is and list the distribution points. Decentralization works well by spreading all the necessary work and responsibilities - allowing maximum effect with minimum effort. We also feel that in maintaining such an open structure we avoid problems of hierarchy - of any one person or group having too much control over the processes of the network.

We hope to encourage new distribution points in any country or area to which the posters would be relevant. At the moment we are largely limited to English language posters but would hope to develop contacts with people interested or involved in parallel or connected structures using other languages. The posters have also been reproduced as stickers, t-shirt designs, grouped together and shown at community art spaces as well as being used as magazine illustrations. In this sense anticopyright functions as a library of radical texts and images. People involved are also very open to collaborating in similar areas. It cannot be over stressed that anticopyright is a continuing project and needs all kinds of involvement from all kinds of people. (See third page for a list of current anticopyright distribution points.)

Brief history

Anticopyright was initially proposed from Cardiff, with a number of leaflets floated around various networks suggesting the idea, listing different ways people could become involved and asking for help and comments. This was accompanied by letters sent direct to people who it was known were producing flyposters themselves or who had numbers of them that were suitable for distribution. This initial process lasted about half a year until sufficient posters had been collected to compile the first catalogue, by then distribution points had also been established in Iowa and Braunschweig (these are no longer going). Once this simple machine had been constructed all that remained was to keep it ticking over through the countless activists, artists, cultural workers and others who pass on information, posters and resources and by doing so produce and enlarge the network.

One effect of the network was to bring into contact a number of groups and individuals who used flyposters on a regular basis in what had previously been a solo endeavour. The network was able to distribute numbers of posters, quite rapidly, to people up and down the country and round the world, when circumstances demanded it. Such posters were produced at the times of the Ambulance Workers' strike, the Gulf War and continually throughout the reign of the ever popular Poll Tax. Obviously this is on a relatively small scale, but working alongside support for the strike, war refusal and non-payment, can bolster and sustain these activities.

D-I-Y

In April 1992 a meeting was held in Stoke-on-Trent which brought together a number of people involved in using, making and distributing the posters. The event proved useful, and achieved its aims of informally encouraging the proliferation of contact and collaboration between people connected with the network. Unlike "proper" arts conferences or whatever there was no massive entrance fee, everyone chipped in what they could afford with food, beer and other costs being shared. We believe that people can do a hell of a lot on low, or no, budgets. Doing it yourself creates a culture responsive to those taking part in it, divests itself of any central authority and enables its perpetual reinvention. This means making and changing politics and culture not because of any party induced political guilt or because it looks good on some arty CV, but because people want to do it, because it responds to our needs and desires.

We hope that this book goes some way in presenting ideas about what is possible, nevertheless, we want more! We want more posters, we want better posters, we want more people getting involved.

Let's wallpaper the world.

Create Spontaneity

ADE·L·VICE '89.

Deny the ritual

WRAP YOUR MEAT

 OR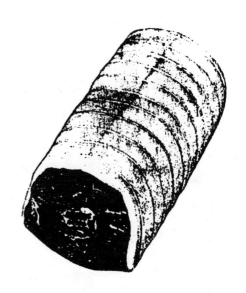

BEAT IT!

FaGaGaGa sez " NO GLOVE, NO LOVE '
please practice safe sex
help stop the spread of AIDS

USE A CONDOM

FaGaGaGa P.O. Box 1382, Youngstown, Ohio 4450(

what if we called a strike and EVERYBODY came?

PERMANENT UNIVERSAL RENT STRIKE

 From Prague to Peoria; up Sydney to Siberia; across Tianimen square to Times Square; EVERYWHERE is fertile ground for a rent strike; for everywhere is the Earth "owned" and thereby devoured by the bulimic behemoth of Capital-Production, vis a vis its methods of diverse genocide.

 STRIKE! Because this condition becomes unbearable. We are, all of us, fully capable of spontaneously, collectively and autonomously rising as one to ride these landlords out of town on a hot rail to Hades.

 STRIKE! For ourselves! Because it is to our advantage to take back the Earth from the slimy tentacles of this commodified monstrosity. We stand to gain our ability to realize ourselves through the liberation of our daily lives.

STRIKE! Because we need more than a good laugh. We need a regular riot.

PLAN DECLARED EFFECTIVE!
begins **1992**

GENITALITY

ANOTHER FATUOUS COMIC

IS A FETISH

DO YOU FEEL

BORED, LONELY, DEPRESSED BY THE SPECTACULAR FATUOUSNESS OF EVERYDAY LIFE?

TELL US ABOUT IT IN THE SQUARE BELOW

☐

not enough space, eh?

well, that's all you're getting for today

this is a fatuous public disservice, in case you hadn't realised

ANOTHER FATUOUS FLYPOSTER FROM THE INSTITUTE OF FATUOUS RESEARCH

Q. How will the election effect the homeless?

A. It won't.

PLEASE NOTE: Homelessness exists **not** because the housing system is not working properly, but because **this is the way that it works.**

NEVER

TRUST

A

POLITICIAN.

THEY ALWAYS LIE.

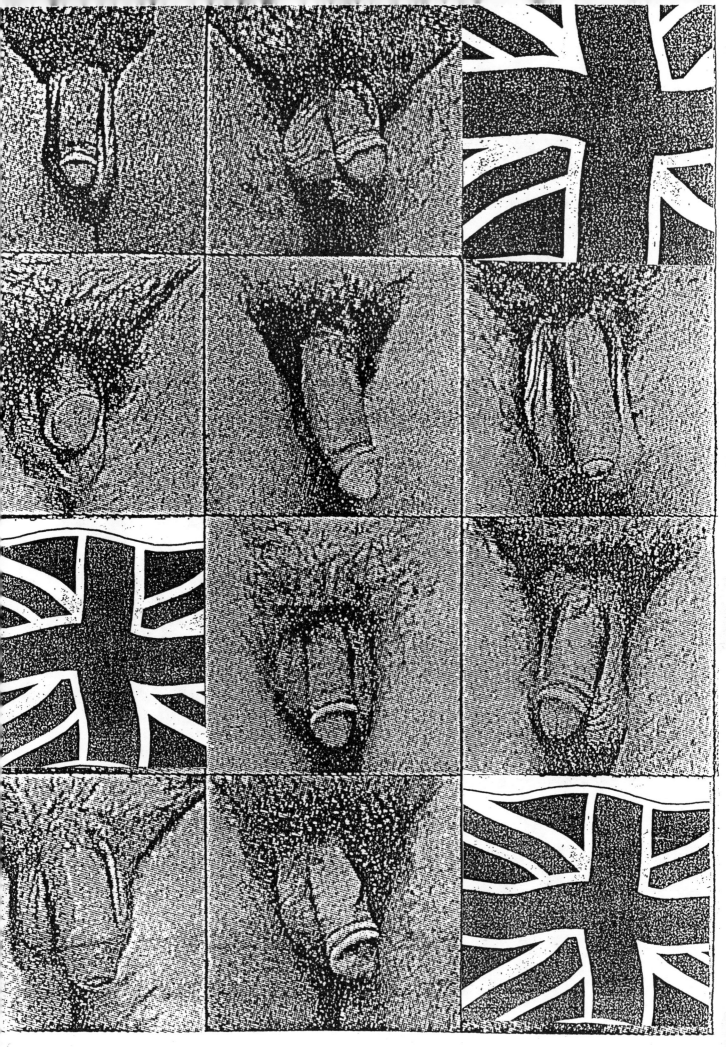

on the rise once again...

SEX (DESIGNED TO MAKE YOU UNZIP)

Calls 34p/min cheap, 45p/min other times.

WELL-HUNG SOCIAL WORKER WANTS IT! 0898 333 825
TOAST MY PANTIES 0898 333 826
SUCK MY NOSE 0898 333 827
MAKE ME A CUP OF TEA 0898 333 828
DAVE'S RAUNCHY POP SOX 0898 333 829
LOVER'S CREMATORIUM FROLIC 0898 333 832
TROT PAPERSELLER RAMS YOUR KETTLE 0898 333 835
MY THUMB YOUR SAUCEPAN 0898 333 836
BENDERBENDER BLENDERMENDER 0898 333 838
TEAM LEADER TOSS UP 0881 888 054
BBIE FOR THREE 0881 888 007
CASEWORKER RAMS IT HOME 0881 888 009
NYMPHO NON SMOKERS SAUCY SOU'WESTER 0881 888 055
DIRECTOR OF SOCIAL SERVICES DEBRIEFING SESSION 0881 888 014
ERUCCA GAMES 0881 888 015
DAVID CASSIDY 0881 888 025
PEEING IN DEAD DOGS EARS 0881 888 026
HACKNEY SQUATTER BATH TIME FANTASY 0881 888 027
OBOE IN MY PANTIES 0898 886 652
SAUCEPAN IN MY DRAWS 0836 405 626
STARFISH MY TURNUPS 0898 800 437
SHAVE MY TANGERINE 0898 886 622
ARBITRARY HOUSEHOLD OBJECT FETISH LINE 0898 886 611
ARBITRARY GENITAL FETISH LINE 0898 800 438
OBJECTIFY MY PARTNER 0836 405 683
CALL MY SEX LINE 0836 405 684
GENITALITY IS A FETISH 0898 886 600

TELEPHONES...TELEPHONES...TELEPHONES...TELEPHO

UNCENSORED STORIES
NO CREDIT CARD NEEDED

Her Royal Highness Princess Anne, Coronation Day, 1953.

Plastic bullets KILL

DO NOT CROSS PICKET LINES.

SOLIDARITY IS STRENGTH.

SCABS ARE SCUM.

WHAT HAPPENS WHEN WE EAT BEEF

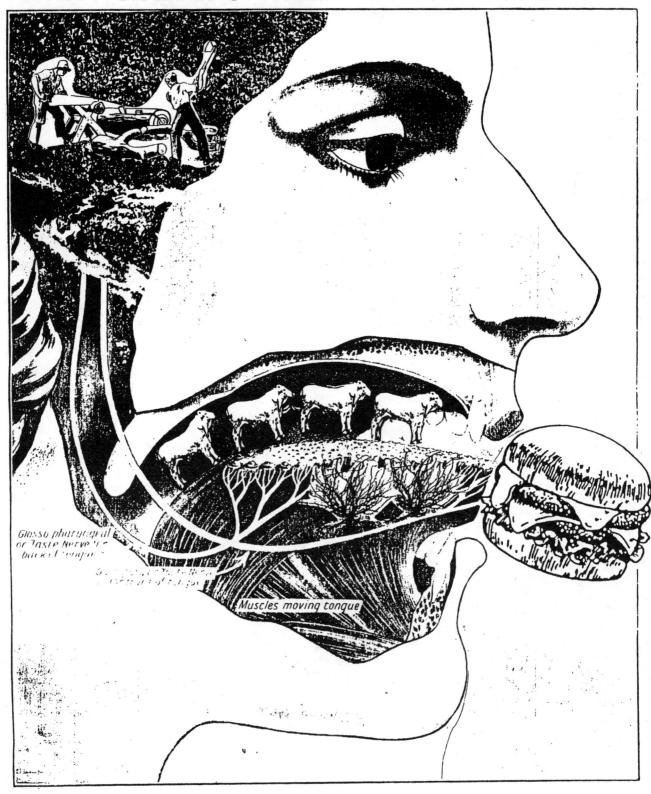

WE CHEW UP RAINFOREST

METROPOLITAN POLICE Appeal for Assistance

SPONSORED BY Coca-Cola

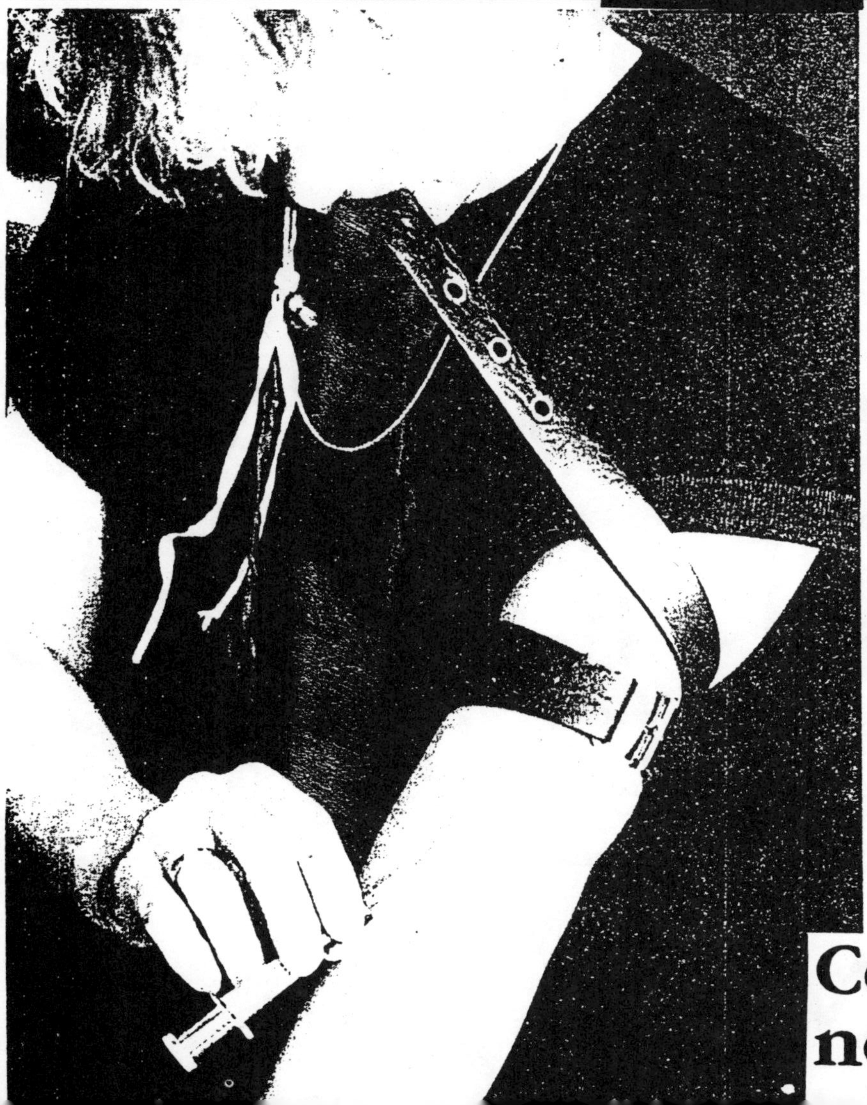

KILL YOUR BOSS

YOUR BOSS IS A PIG.
DO YOURSELF A FAVOUR
AND KILL HIM/HER.
THE THEORY OF US PLAYING A
LEARNING GAME CAN ONLY BE
ENFORCED BY INTRAVENOUS
DRUG USAGE AND THE SLAUGHTER
OF INNOCENT SCUM.

THE ASSOCIATION FOR IMPROVING
THE CONDITION OF THE FOLLOWERS
OF LUCIFER AND ANTICHRIST AND
THE SOCIETY FOR LUCKY LAMBS.

Comrades, we're not the future,

Tel:- 0*********

DEMOCRACY, TRUTH, LAW, NATION, EDUCATION, HERO, POLITICS, RELIGION, CAREER.

ALL THESE WORDS ARE USED TO CONDITION YOU, BUT DON'T BELIEVE US, WE USE THEM TOO!

WE HAVE FOUND NEW HOMES FOR THE RICH

BRINGING THE GAS TO THE CUSTOMER'S DOOR

We would like to thank the following for helping to keep this child hungry

"Hunger" is a registered product of multinational corporations, operating in conjunction with all governments.

WORK RATE TOO FAST
(APPLY RESISTANCE)

HOW FIT IS YOUR BRAIN?

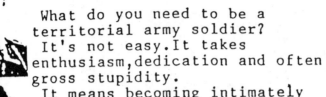

What do you need to be a territorial army soldier?
It's not easy. It takes enthusiasm, dedication and often gross stupidity.
It means becoming intimately acquainted with the self loading rifle to make killing someone part of your job satisfaction.
The territorial army works alongside both the Regular Army and the NATO forces
Which is why we're not too fussy about who joins. You see we're not really bothered who gets killed as long as it's not us. We now even let blacks in the army, see the token black man in this advert, second down on the left. You may have a hard time in the barracks but that's not our concern. It doesn't matter to us what colour a bullet catcher is.
You even get paid equivalent rates to the Regulars. What more do you want? Blood? That can be arranged too, along with a free wooden cross on a island in the South Atlantic.
Interested? Dumb enough? Cut out the coupon. Who knows, you could make the Six O'clock news by this time next year.

GIVE BLOOD-JOIN THE ARMY.

THE TERRITORIAL ARMY.
Freepost 4335 (Dept. DE23/2B) Bristol BS1 3YX.
Please send me further information on the T.A.
Name_____
Address_____
_____ Age (17½-32)_____
READY AND WAITING - 0800 555 555 (FREE).
The Armed Forces are equal opportunity employers under the terms of the Race Relations Act 1976.

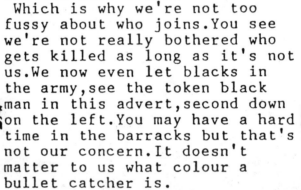

WE'RE HERE

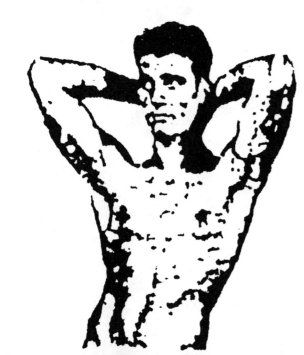

WE'RE QUEER

GET USED TO IT

Parked cars get stolen - Don't stop

Pedestrians attack cars in this area

SOUTH AFRICA IS LIKE A VICIOUS WOLF,

OPENLY HOSTILE TOWARDS BLACK HUMANITY.

AMERICA IS CUNNING LIKE A FOX, FRIENDLY AND SMILING,

BUT EVEN MORE VICIOUS AND DEADLY THAN THE WOLF.

THE WOLF,FOX AND COYOTE ARE ENEMIES OF HUMANITY;

ALL THREE ARE CANINE,

ALL THREE HUMILIATE AND MUTILATE THEIR VICTIMS;

ALL THREE HAVE THE SAME OBJECTIVES,

                    BUT DIFFER ONLY IN METHODS.

LIBERTY AND JUSTICE FOR ALL*

*Offer not available to anyone with AIDS

ART IS NOT A MIRROR HELD UP TO REALITY BUT A HAMMER WITH WHICH TO SHAPE IT.

BERTOLT BRECHT

T he hottest places in hell are reserved for those who, in time of great moral crisis, maintain their neutrality.

Dante 1265-1321

Come Share Our Values

FREE! Separation

Brain wash — Original or Peppermint — $3.99 quart cont.

Misery — 1-lb Pkg — $1.39

Meaningless Existence — Frozen - lb — 49¢

angst — 100 foot roll — $1.79

Boredom — $2.99 lb. — USDA CHOICE

As civilisation advances into oblivion, so too do its adherents become more and more oblivious to the miserable conditions of the situation.

Images — 1-lb Bag — 89¢

Armor — 48-oz ctnr — $2.59

Masks — pkg of 6 — $1.69

We suggest that this denial is a normal defensive response to the pain brought on by the process of reducing every nuance of your miraculous life to an empty abstract value.

Cancer — 12-oz Can — $1.49

Confusion — 2 10-oz Pkgs of 12 — $1.09

Breakfast Favorite **Impotence** — 8 in pkg — $1.59

Domestication — "OUR OWN" Made Fresh Daily — $3.59 4 oz. cont.

Delicious Iced **Stress** — 2 in pkg — $1.09

Cinnamon Cheese **Death** — each — $2.09

Our Fake of the Month! **Freedom** — each — $1.39

Why not mourn the loss of joy? Get together with friends or go alone to the local corporate grocer and ask where these sale items can be found. Check the gas stations. Inquire at the chamber of commerce. Write to your statesmen. These bargains can be found everywhere.

"The last ramparts of the sacred are tottering. If we demolish them rapidly we shall bring a world to an end. If we do not, humanity will be crushed beneath them as they fall." -- Vaneigem

Alienation — Party Size — 12 for $1.09

ELEUTHEROS PROD
P.O. Box 141
Bearsville, NY 12409

GO BERSERK

STARTING NOW!

(speech bubbles, clockwise from top)

When humans began to organise life into an economic system of commodity exchange, the spirit of life began to leave this place, and we began a journey through misery. I say this journey is over. I say we take off our armor and come out to play.

The only art left that has any redeeming value is the art of liberation, revolution and ecstatic love, which dismantles the basis of today's social arrangements.

Yes, for too long have we sacrificed our pleasure for the sake of Production & Development. Those who have a vested interest in maintaining this arrangement appear to wield a great power over us, yet this appearance is but cheap art. It is you & I who have maintained this arrangement mainly by performing our appointed tasks on a regular daily basis. It is you & I who can do away with such arrangements.

They'll foolishly label us as Utopians in a vain effort to ridicule and recuperate our ideas. Why? Because we are a threat. We play outside of the realms of power, beyond the influence of terror and other tactics of coercion.

Remember! As you dismantle the instruments of wreckage and alienation — keep your heart open! Let the force of wild life flow through you! Cum, cum! Let's be going!

FREEDOM

Bedlam Press — A post-Sub-Genial Organisation.

SHRIEK WHEN THE PAIN HITS DURING INTERROGATION. REACH INTO THE DARK AGES TO FIND A SOUND THAT IS LIQUID HORROR, A SOUND OF THE BRINK WHERE MAN STOPS AND THE BEAST AND NAMELESS CRUEL FORCES BEGIN. SCREAM WHEN YOUR LIFE IS THREATENED. FORM A NOISE SO TRUE THAT YOUR TORMENTOR RECOGNIZES IT AS A VOICE THAT LIVES IN HIS OWN THROAT. THE TRUE SOUND TELLS HIM THAT HE CUTS HIS FLESH WHEN HE CUTS YOURS, THAT HE CANNOT THRIVE AFTER HE TORTURES YOU. SCREAM THAT HE DESTROYS ALL KINDNESS IN YOU AND BLACKENS EVERY VISION YOU COULD HAVE SHOWN HIM.

DON'T TALK DOWN TO ME. DON'T BE POLITE TO ME. DON'T TRY TO MAKE ME FEEL NICE. DON'T RELAX. I'LL CUT THE SMILE OFF YOUR FACE. YOU THINK I DON'T KNOW WHAT'S GOING ON. YOU THINK I'M AFRAID TO REACT. THE JOKE'S ON YOU. I'M BIDING MY TIME, LOOKING FOR THE SPOT. YOU THINK NO ONE CAN REACH YOU, NO ONE CAN HAVE WHAT YOU HAVE. I'VE BEEN PLANNING WHILE YOU'RE PLAYING. I'VE BEEN SAVING WHILE YOU'RE SPENDING. THE GAME IS ALMOST OVER SO IT'S TIME YOU ACKNOWLEDGE ME. DO YOU WANT TO FALL NOT EVER KNOWING WHO TOOK YOU?

COMMIES ᴀʀᴇ CHRIST WANT YOU!

无产阶级革命派在毛泽东思想的伟大红旗下联合起来！
无产阶级革命派在毛泽东思想的伟大红旗下联合起来！

In the forthcoming elections....

VOTE FOR NOBODY

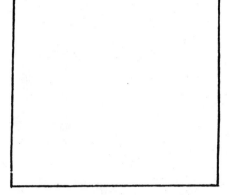

Election-time is here again and we're being brow-beaten to take part. But most people, quite rightly, feel that all the Parties are the same - in it for their own power. They are convinced that all Candidates are irrelevant to their real problems and situation. NOBODY is different...

<u>NOBODY</u> WILL MAKE SURE EVERYONE HAS ALL THEY NEED
<u>NOBODY</u> WILL ENSURE DECENT HOMES FOR ALL
<u>NOBODY</u> WILL CREATE A GOOD ENVIRONMENT
<u>NOBODY</u> WILL PUT THE POWER BACK INTO THE HANDS
OF ORDINARY PEOPLE

Isn't this all just commonsense? <u>Your</u> feelings, <u>your</u> needs and <u>your</u> potential to organise and act are constantly undermined by all the Parties that exist. They only con and manipulate people in order to get influence for themselves. NOBODY believes in <u>you</u>....

NOBODY CAN DO FOR YOU
WHAT YOU SHOULD DO FOR YOURSELVES

so....

VOTE FOR NOBODY
—you know it makes sense

IF NOBODY GETS IN IT'LL BE MUCH BETTER FOR ALL OF US

Come the election results, if most people vote for Nobody, we call on people to seize control of the Town Halls and all local services and resources. Support eachother.

Together (with Nobody leading us) we can change <u>our</u> world

---

<u>Real</u> politics is alive wherever people organise and act for themselves - strikes, protests, self-help groups, solidarity and caring for eachother...refusing to obey, to pay. Our world and our lives are being destroyed - FIGHT BACK NOW.

remember

violent nonobjectiveness

MUGGERS

This is a working-class area

Get the Rich Instead!

RITUAL ABUSE IS RIFE

IN YOUR AREA

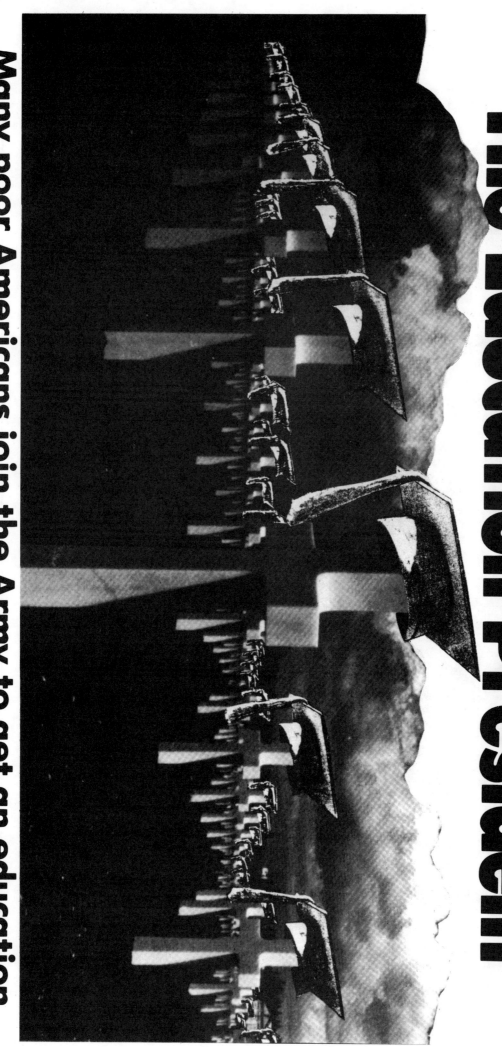

George Bush, "The Education President"

Many poor Americans join the Army to get an education and a better life. If Bush had a real policy for public education, who would fight his wars?

trust your desires.

"They have to be constantly watched," said the employers' newspaper, *Textile World*," or they will go from bad to worse in order to make more time for play."

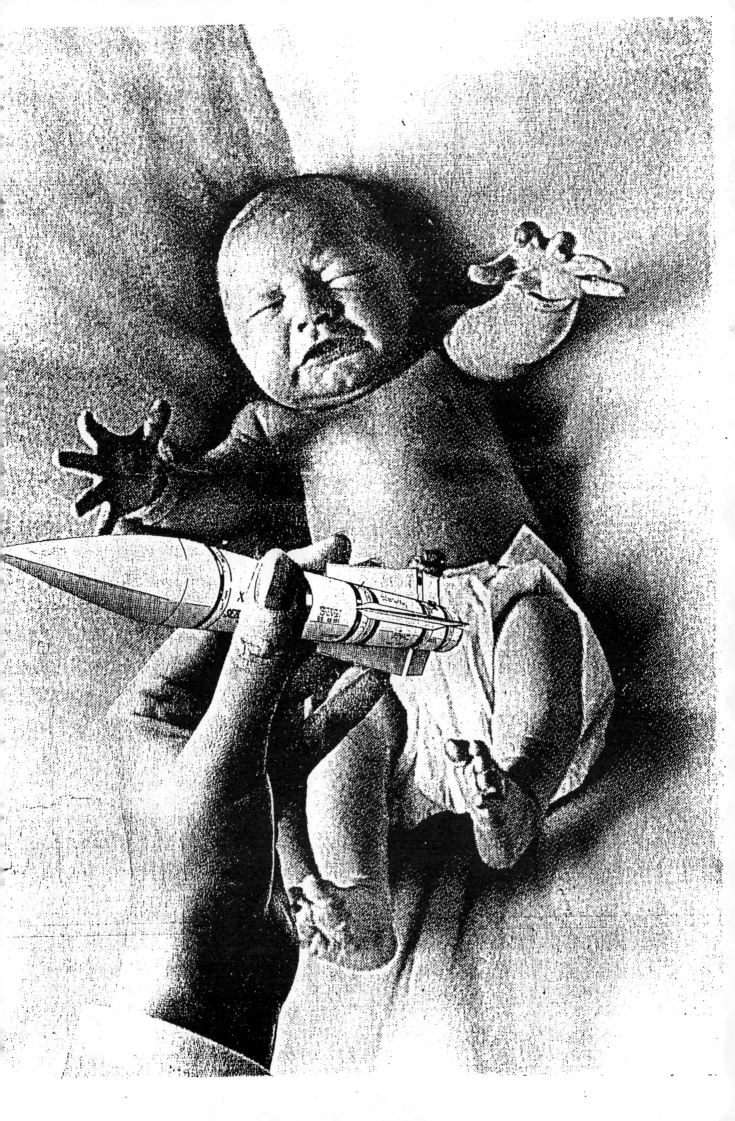

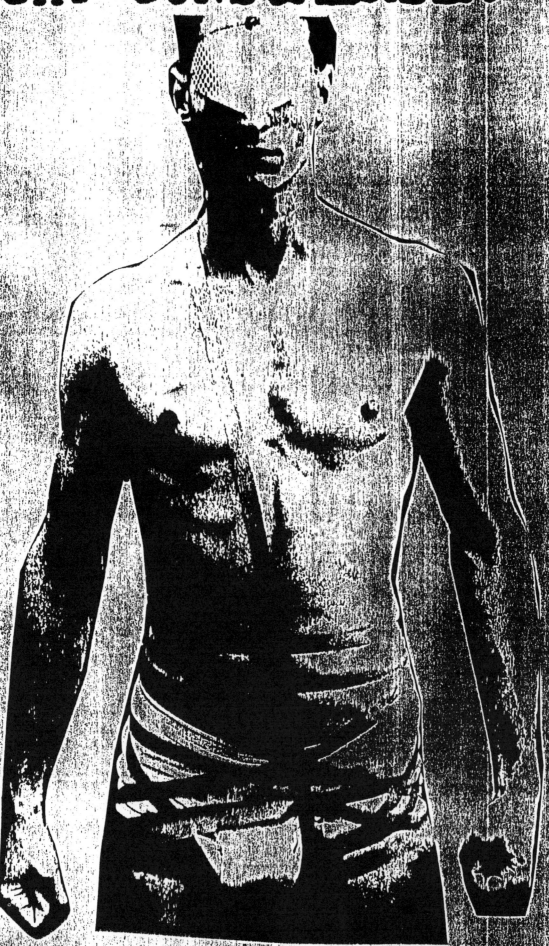

Today everything is visible—no part of the spectacle remains hidden. Fading illusions are so many targets ranged around those of us enraged by our cramped existence; so many delicious inducements to unleash the weapons of mockery and laughter.

There is not a single part of this repressive totality against which critical intelligence cannot direct itself. Always faithful to the passions of the person who wields it, here it undermines technology, there exposes time, here again assaults work and its imposed "necessity".

This method is the surest way to help arouse a spontaneous, uncontrolled insurrection, whose global unfolding would plunge the revolutionary into a delirium intense enough, lucid enough, to procure for him/her the sweetest pleasures offered by life.

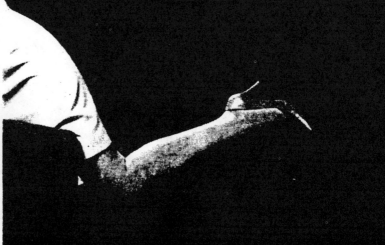

Anti-Authoritarians Anonymous   P.O. Box 11331   Eugene, OR 97440

THE HELPING HAND OF WESTERN MULTINATIONALS.

GUY FAWKES

The only person to enter Parliament with honest intentions

Fun.

Lifestyles.

Careers.

Clothes.

Write Your Will Now!

What's wrong with McDonald's? Everything they don't want you to know.

SOME FACTS TO CHEW ON WITH YOUR BIG MAC

800 SQUARE MILES OF FOREST A YEAR ARE DESTROYED TO PACKAGE THEIR PRODUCTS. THESE FORESTS PRODUCE HALF THE AIR WE BREATHE!

48 PER CENT OF A QUARTER POUNDER'S WEIGHT IS WATER, NO WONDER YOU'RE STILL HUNGRY.

THE PIGS AND CHICKENS THEY ELECTROCUTE AND KNIFE SPEND ALL THEIR EXISTENCE IN CONCRETE CELLS WITH NO DAYLIGHT. HEALTHY?? REALLY THAT HUNGRY???

BOYCOTT  AND LIVE Take control of your Life.

"All this for nothing?"

Yes.

At Sainsbury's we know that good food has never been more important. Today's diet means less meat and dairy products, and fewer chemicals. That's good news for us, good news for other animals, and good news for the earth.

Fortunately good food has never been cheaper. For several years Sainsbury's have pioneered a new concept in consumer-choice. We call it SHOPPING WITHOUT MONEY. The idea is simple: food is a right, not a privilege. And we know that making millions by selling food, while three-quarters of the world starve, is immoral. All the more so, since those who make food, package it, transport it and sell it are usually overworked and underpaid.

Our answer is quite simple: under the SHOPPING WITHOUT MONEY scheme, if you see something you want, just take it. Some might call it shoplifting. We prefer to think of it as you taking back what is yours.

Good food costs nothing at Sainsbury'

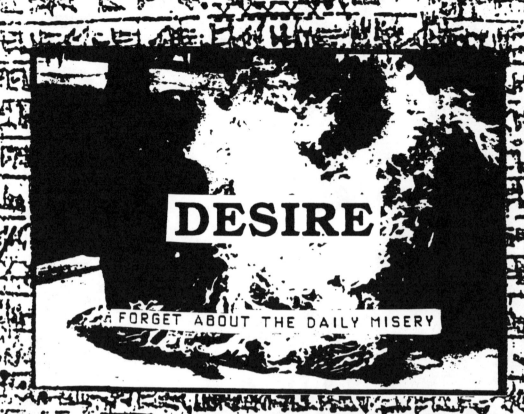

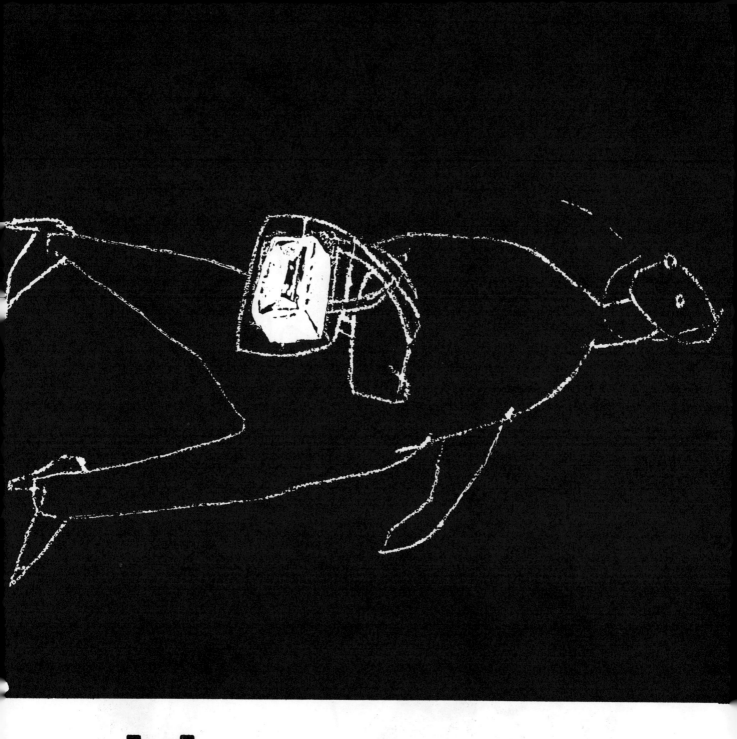

I'VE GOT MINE.

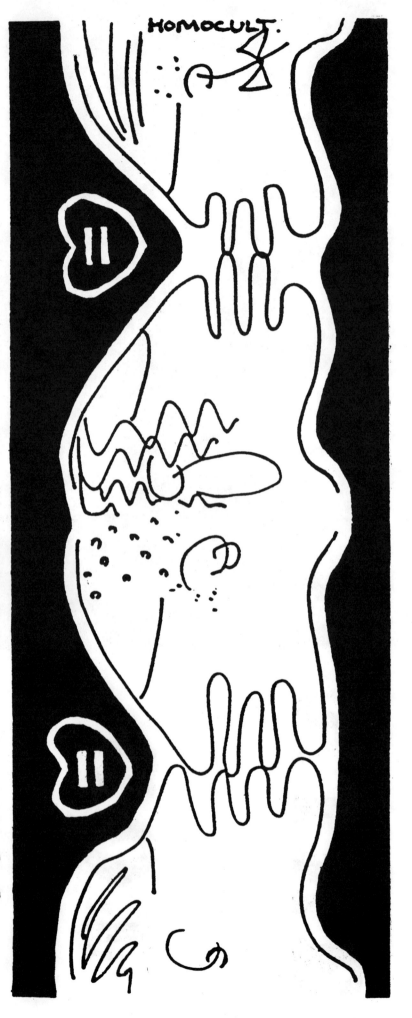

HOMOCULTURE
OUR LANGUAGE IS PERVERSION
CORRUPTION RECLAIMING ACTING
CHANGING SURVIVING SUBVERTING
EVOLVING LIFE

HETROTRASH
THEIR LANGUAGE IS CONSERVING
STAGNATING LINGERING DEATH

QUEER
ALL WHICH WAS SAID TO BE GOOD
WAS WRONG, EVIL WAS OUR FRIEND
ALL ALONG. THEY MADE US BELIEVE
IN OUR OWN SELF HATE.

LOVE YOURSELF
COMMON QUEER NIGGER BITCH

OUR WORLD
THE WORLD OF THE MANY
INSULTED BY THE FEW...

SHAME
RICH GAYS PLAY DEAD

ROUGH QUEERS LIVE
REBEL CREATE RIOT FUCK.

THEIR STYLE
MINDLESS MONEY FLAT CONSUMING GLOSS

OUR STYLE
STOLEN CHEAP BENT FILTH

LOOK OUT

OTHER PUBLICATIONS FROM WORKING PRESS

CROSSING BLACK WATERS
Edited by Allan de Souza & Shaheen Merali
ISBN 1 870736 21 4. £8.50.

Crossing Black Waters refers to Kala Pani the black oceans surrounding the Indian subcontinent. To cross them was to break with tradition, to break ones caste - literally to become an outcast.
Accompanying a major exhibition of the same name, the book looks at the work of fourteen South Asian artists - eight based in Britain and six in the subcontinent. Through essays, photographs and interviews *Crossing Black Waters* analyses the artists' handling of the colonial legacy and their attempts to extend and develop a contemporary cultural practice.

ON COMMON GROUND
Francis Reed
ISBN 1 870736 27 3. £5.80

A sparkling look at the history and future of ground space, peoples' space, in England. Taking the "remote and fortifying Commons" as the starting point, this book is about the space and society from which architecture grows.

POSTCARDS FROM POLAND and other correspondences
Maria Jastrebska and Jola Scicinska
ISBN 1 870736 06 0. £6.95.

In this book the authors tell of their recent trip "home" to Poland. Maria's moving poetry is illustrated throughout with stunning reproductions of Jola Scicinska's traditional papercuts. Both Jola and Maria are Jewish and lesbian, their poems and pictures often address the tensions between faith, sexuality and national identity in a unique format.

IF COMIX: "MENTAL"
Limited edition of 1500 with poster and record. £4.50.

Britain's first computer generated comic.
"For a great many working class artists 'Fine Art' is a redundant medium which can only collude with injustice through its ability to make the ruling class feel civilised. The comic format is an alternative." (Graham Harwood)

FIST

FIST 4. £2.49.

This issue of the libertarian megazine includes interviews and photos with Z'ev (metal anarchic shaman), Alain Jourgensen (electro punk of Ministry, 1000 Homo DJs, Revolting Cocks), Sol Invictus (ex Death in June/Crisis), Tom Vague (Post Punk writer), Christina Berry (leather S/M sculptor), Tina (S/M ritualist). Plus the well known mix of hard hitting graphics and stories.

THE STATE OF THE ART AND THE ART OF THE STATE
Conrad Atkinson
ISBN 1 870730736 14 1. £2.95.

Originally conceived as one of the Power lectures given in several Australian cities in 1983. It was first edited and published by the Australian feminist journal LIP in 1984. Now amended and with a new introduction. Followed by a bibliography and CV. "The production of culture and its mediation in the hegemony of the state."

IN YOUR BLOOD football culture in the late eighties and early nineties.
Richard Turner
ISBN 1 870736 07 9. £4.95.

In Your Blood takes a general look at the lifestyle of fans on the terraces. It suggests that a particular culture has developed among football fans which is a particularly dynamic element of working class culture. Football is a way of life to many people, one that is well worth defending against incompetent management, spiteful government legislation, greedy developers and media hysteria.

CLASS MYTHS AND CULTURE
Stefan Szczelkun
ISBN 1 870736 03 6. £5.95.

Passionate essays on; the oppression of artists, the myth of being lower middle class, glamour as an embodiment of class separation and how an urban working class architecture was nipped in the bud. These concise essays are followed by reports of the strange and inspiring cultural events that Szczelkun has devised in order to put his ideas into practice.

NOTHING SPECIAL
Written and illustrated by Micheline Mason
ISBN 1 870736 02 8. £2.50.

"I use and electric wheelchair. I cannot speak very clearly or eat, or go to the toilet without help. I am doing fine."
An eight year old girl describes a day at her local primary school. Although at least a quarter of the school have disabilities or learning difficulties, she says her school is "Nothing Special…"